The Ultimate Steak Cookbook

Mouthwatering Steak Recipes You Can't Get Enough Of

BY: SOPHIA FREEMAN

© 2020 Sophia Freeman All Rights Reserved

★★★★★★★★★★★★

Liability

This publication is meant as an informational tool. The individual purchaser accepts all liability if damages occur because of following the directions or guidelines set out in this publication. The Author bears no responsibility for reparations caused by the misuse or misinterpretation of the content.

Copyright

The content of this publication is solely for entertainment purposes and is meant to be purchased by one individual. Permission is not given to any individual who copies, sells or distributes parts or the whole of this publication unless it is explicitly given by the Author in writing.

* * * * ★ ★ ★ ★ ★ * * *

Table of Contents

Introduction 7

Additional Interesting & Useful Information 9

    Pepper Steak 10

    Steak Strips with Chimichurri 13

    Grilled Flank Steak 16

    Filet Mignon with Balsamic Sauce 19

    Garlic Steak 22

    Steak with Garlic Butter 25

    Blue Cheese Filet Mignon 28

    Barbecue Flank Steak 32

    Swiss Steak 35

    Grilled Rib Eye Steak 38

    Mojo Steak 41

    Beer Steaks 44

    Country-Style Steak 47

    Slow-Cooked London Broil 50

Slow Cooked Round Steak 53

Filet Mignon with Mustard Sauce 56

Rib Eye Steak with Ginger Soy 59

Ginger Steak 62

Caribbean Beef Loin 65

Salsa Steak 68

Peppercorn Steak 71

Steak Strips in Mushroom Sauce 74

Barbecue Buttered Steaks 77

Irish Steaks 80

Steak in Marsala Sauce 83

Steak with Mushroom Tarragon 86

Adobo Steak 89

Korean Steak 92

Flank Steak Rolls 95

New York Steak 98

Bacon-Wrapped Filet Mignon with Peppercorn Sauce 101

Steak Sauerbraten 105

Steak with Red Wine Sauce 108

Bourbon Strip Steak 111

Chicago-Style Steak 114

Thyme Steaks with Mushrooms 117

Koji Steak 120

Roasted Steak 123

Sweet Savory Steak 126

Rib Eye Steaks with Bell Peppers 129

Italian Rib Eye 132

Grilled Steak with Strawberry Sauce 135

Indian Steak 138

Coffee Steaks 141

Garlic Rosemary Prime Rib 144

Steak with Broccoli Rabe Peas 147

Flank Steak with Tomato Salad 150

Herbed Steak with Tomatoes 153

Seared Steak with Crispy Herbs 156

Flank Steak with Corn Butter 159

Conclusion 162

About the Author 163

Author's Afterthoughts 164

Introduction

The origin of the term 'steak' comes from the Old Norse words, "stickna" which means 'be roasted' and "steikja" which means 'to roast on a spit'.

The earliest usage of the term in literature was through a 15th-century cookbook.

Steak can be cooked in a variety of ways beginning from the most basic, which is by applying high heat over a gas or charcoal grill.

Pan-seared steak is done with a cast iron or stainless steel skillet on a stove. It is usually cooked with butter and some herbs.

The sous vide method involves sealing the marinated meat in airtight bags and cooked on a water bath. Then, the meat is seared in a pan or grilled before serving.

The traditional sear method is where you brown the surfaces to seal all the savory juices, then finish in the oven to cook nicely.

While the reverse-sear is just the opposite of the traditional sear method and entails a longer cooking time.

Excited to give these methods a try?

Let's get started!

Additional Interesting & Useful Information

- Indeed, letting the steak rest for a few minutes after cooking will improve the overall taste and texture.
- Although the finger test is an easy way to tell doneness, a reliable meat thermometer is your best bet in getting your steaks perfectly done each time.
- Rare steaks cook at 120 degrees F with the outside slightly browned. They are mostly raw and bloody with a bright red and soft texture at the center.
- Medium rare steaks have an internal temperature of 130 degrees F. They cook about a minute longer than rare and have a warm red color in the middle.
- Medium steaks are slightly firmer to the touch than that of medium rare and cook with an internal temperature of 140 degrees F. Apparently, the outside has a rich brown color while in their center is a light pink band.
- Medium well steaks still have a hint of pale pink but are mostly gray-brown in the middle. They are firmer than medium steaks and cook at an internal temperature of 150 degrees F.
- Well-done steaks are typically drier and tougher due to the longer cooking time. They are cooked through and through, have no hint of pink in the middle, and have a charred surface. They cook via slow heat with an internal temperature of 160 degrees F and up.

Pepper Steak

Pepper steak is said to have originated in Central America and the Caribbean. It is made with sliced beef marinated in sweet savory sauce and simmered with bell peppers until tender. This is literally the kind of steak dish that will easily become a staple at your home.

Serving Size: 4

Preparation Cooking Time: 50 minutes

Ingredients:

- 1 onion, sliced
- 2 cloves garlic, minced
- 1 red bell pepper, nicely sliced into thick strips
- 1 green bell pepper, nicely sliced into thick strips
- 2 tablespoons olive oil
- ¼ cup red wine vinegar
- ¼ cup honey
- ¼ cup soy sauce
- 1 lb. beef, sliced into strips

Instructions:

1. Pour the olive oil into your pan over medium heat.

2. Cook the onion, garlic and bell pepper for 1 to 2 minutes, stirring frequently.

3. Transfer to a plate.

4. Increase the heat to medium high.

5. Pour in the honey, red wine vinegar and soy sauce.

6. Mix well.

7. Stir in the beef.

8. Bring to a boil.

9. Reduce heat and simmer for 30 minutes.

10. Add the onion mixture.

11. Cook for another 10 minutes.

Nutrients per Serving:

- Calories: 387.5
- Fat: 19.2 g
- Saturated Fat: 6.1 g
- Carbohydrates: 33 g
- Fiber: 2.1 g
- Protein: 22.6 g
- Cholesterol: 53.6 mg
- Sugars: 27.2 g
- Sodium: 1259.5 mg
- Potassium: 526.2 mg

Steak Strips with Chimichurri

Chimichurri refers to a popular sauce and condiment in Uruguay and Argentina that is made by combining olive oil, red wine vinegar, minced parsley, minced garlic and oregano. Pair your grilled steak strips with this sauce and for sure, the dish will be a hit in the dinner table.

Serving Size: 4

Preparation Cooking Time: 25 minutes

Ingredients:

- 1 lb. beef sirloin, sliced into strips
- 1 tablespoon vegetable oil
- Salt and pepper to taste
- ½ cup olive oil
- ¼ cup red wine vinegar
- 1 onion, chopped
- 3 cloves garlic, minced
- 1 cup Italian parsley (flat leaf)
- 1 tablespoon dried oregano
- 2 tablespoons smoked paprika
- 2 tablespoons chipotle peppers in adobo sauce

Instructions:

1. Preheat your grill and grease the grate.

2. Coat the steak strips with the vegetable oil.

3. Sprinkle with the salt and pepper.

4. Grill the steak strips for 3 minutes per side.

5. In a bowl, mix the remaining ingredients.

6. Lastly, serve the steak with the chimichurri on the side, or spread it on top of the steak before serving.

Nutrients per Serving:

- Calories: 189.9
- Fat: 20.3 g
- Saturated Fat: 2.8 g
- Carbohydrates: 2.2 g
- Fiber: 0.4 g
- Protein: 0.5 g
- Sugars: 0.3 g
- Cholesterol: 0 mg
- Sodium: 296.3 mg
- Potassium: 70.2 mg

Grilled Flank Steak

This marinated flank steak is bursting with flavors. It's juicy, tender, and truly delicious. Make this recipe at home that takes minimal active effort.

Serving Size: 6

Preparation Cooking Time: 6 hours and 30 minutes

Ingredients:

- 2 cloves garlic, minced
- ½ cup vegetable oil
- ¼ cup red wine vinegar
- 1 ½ tablespoons Worcestershire sauce
- 2 tablespoons freshly squeezed lemon juice
- 1/3 cup soy sauce
- 1 tablespoon Dijon mustard
- Pepper to taste
- 1 ½ lb. flank steak

Instructions:

1. Combine the garlic, vegetable oil, lemon juice, red wine vinegar, Worcestershire sauce, soy sauce, Dijon mustard and pepper in a bowl.

2. Add the meat to the bowl.

3. Coat the meat with the marinade.

4. Next, cover the bowl and marinate in the refrigerator for 6 hours.

5. Preheat your grill.

6. Cook the steak on the grill for 5 minutes per side.

Nutrients per Serving:

- Calories: 275
- Fat: 22.5 g
- Carbohydrates: 3.4 g
- Fiber: 0.2 g
- Protein: 14.8 g
- Saturated Fat: 4 g
- Cholesterol: 27 mg
- Sugars: 1 g
- Sodium: 935 mg
- Potassium: 245 mg

Filet Mignon with Balsamic Sauce

Actually, want a fancy dinner but don't want to spend too much time in the kitchen? Consider preparing this recipe—filet mignon steaks glazed with balsamic sauce and served with steamed beans and roasted potatoes.

Serving Size: 2

Preparation Cooking Time: 20 minutes

Ingredients:

- 8 oz. beef tenderloin
- Salt and pepper to taste
- ¼ cup red wine
- ¼ cup balsamic vinegar
- Steamed green beans
- Roasted baby potatoes

Instructions:

1. First, season both sides of the meat with the salt and pepper.

2. Second, place a pan over medium high heat.

3. Next, add the steak and cook for 1 minute per side.

4. Reduce heat and stir in the red wine and balsamic vinegar.

5. Cook approximately for 4 to 5 minutes per side.

6. Pour the glaze over the steaks.

7. Serve with the green beans and roasted baby potatoes.

Nutrients per Serving:

- Calories: 366.6
- Fat: 26.2 g
- Saturated Fat: 10.6 g
- Carbohydrates: 5.7 g
- Fiber: 0.1 g
- Protein: 20.3 g
- Cholesterol: 80.5 mg
- Sugars: 4.6 g
- Sodium: 63.5 mg
- Potassium: 402.3 mg

Garlic Steak

This garlic steak is too good to resist. Marinated in a mixture of soy sauce, honey, garlic, vinegar, liquid smoke and cayenne pepper, the steak comes out tender, juicy and flavorful.

Serving Size: 2

Preparation Cooking Time: 1 day and 15 minutes

Ingredients:

- 3 tablespoons garlic
- 2 tablespoons olive oil
- ½ cup balsamic vinegar
- 2 tablespoons honey
- ¼ cup soy sauce
- 1 teaspoon Worcestershire sauce
- 1 teaspoon onion powder
- ½ teaspoon liquid smoke
- Pinch cayenne pepper
- Salt and pepper to taste
- 2 rib eye steaks

Instructions:

1. Mix the garlic, olive oil, balsamic vinegar, soy sauce, Worcestershire sauce, liquid smoke, onion powder, cayenne pepper, honey, salt and pepper in a bowl.

2. Place the steaks in a baking dish.

3. Pour the marinade over the steaks and coat evenly.

4. Cover with foil.

5. Marinate in the refrigerator for 1 day.

6. When ready to cook, preheat your grill.

7. Grill the rib eye steaks for 6 to 7 minutes per side.

Nutrients per Serving:

- Calories: 576.4
- Fat: 36 g
- Saturated Fat: 10.6 g
- Carbohydrates: 36 g
- Fiber: 1.2 g
- Protein: 28.4 g
- Cholesterol: 81.2 mg
- Sugars: 27.4 g
- Sodium: 2496.5 mg
- Potassium: 585.6 mg

Steak with Garlic Butter

Adding garlic butter sauce to steak is one of the most popular ways to prepare steak. This is a melt-in-your-mouth delicious steak recipe you'd surely want to enjoy over and over.

Serving Size: 8

Preparation Cooking Time: 30 minutes

Ingredients:

- ½ cup butter
- 5 cloves garlic, crushed and minced
- 2 teaspoons garlic powder
- 4 lb. beef sirloin steak
- Salt and pepper to taste

Instructions:

1. Preheat your grill.

2. In a pan over medium low heat, add the butter, garlic and garlic powder.

3. Season the steak with the salt and pepper.

4. Next, grill the steak for 3 to 5 minutes per side.

5. Pour the butter sauce on top of the steak.

6. Let rest for 3 minutes before serving.

Nutrients per Serving:

- Calories: 453
- Fat: 32.2 g
- Saturated Fat: 16 g
- Cholesterol: 151 mg
- Sugars: 0 g
- Carbohydrates: 1 g
- Fiber: 0.1 g
- Protein: 37.7 g
- Sodium: 167 mg
- Potassium: 509 mg

Blue Cheese Filet Mignon

This blue cheese filet mignon steak recipe takes more steps than the other recipes you'll find in this book. But the result is literally worth all the time and effort.

Serving Size: 4

Preparation Cooking Time: 50 minutes

Ingredients:

- 1 tablespoon butter
- ½ cup white onion, chopped
- 3 cloves garlic, raw
- 1 tablespoon thyme
- 1 tablespoon oil
- ¾ cup reduced-sodium beef broth
- ½ cup port wine
- 4 beef tenderloins
- ¾ cup blue cheese
- ¼ cup breadcrumbs

Instructions:

1. First, add the butter to a pan over medium heat.

2. Cook the onion and garlic for 1 minute.

3. Stir in the thyme.

4. Cook for another 2 minutes.

5. Pour in the broth and wine.

6. Next, scrape the bottom of the pan using a wooden spoon.

7. Bring to a boil.

8. Cook the mixture until liquid has been reduced to about half a cup.

9. Transfer the mixture to a bowl. Then, set aside.

10. Preheat your oven to 350 degrees F.

11. Pour the oil in a pan over medium high heat.

12. Sear the steaks for 1 to 2 minutes.

13. Transfer the steaks to a baking pan.

14. Roast the steaks for 15 minutes.

15. In a bowl, mix the blue cheese and breadcrumbs.

16. Spread the blue cheese mixture on top of the steaks.

17. Broil for 4 to 5 minutes.

18. Serve with the wine sauce.

Nutrients per Serving:

- Calories: 402.2
- Fat: 27.8 g
- Saturated Fat: 12.5 g
- Carbohydrates: 9 g
- Fiber: 0.5 g
- Protein: 24.5 g
- Cholesterol: 84.7 mg
- Sugars: 1.4 g
- Sodium: 462.6 mg
- Potassium: 423.6 mg

Barbecue Flank Steak

To save time and effort, you can certainly prepare this recipe using prepared barbecue sauce. But if you want your steak recipe completely homemade, you can also make your own barbecue sauce.

Serving Size: 6

Preparation Cooking Time: 8 hours and 30 minutes

Ingredients:

- ½ cup corn or vegetable oil
- 3 tablespoons honey
- 2 tablespoons distilled vinegar
- ¼ cup soy sauce
- ½ teaspoon garlic powder
- ½ teaspoon ground ginger
- 1 ½ lb. flank steak

Instructions:

1. Add the oil, honey, vinegar, soy sauce, garlic powder and ground ginger in a food processor.

2. Pulse until fully combined.

3. Add the steak to a baking pan.

4. Pierce the steak using a fork.

5. Add the honey mixture to the pan.

6. Coat the steak with this mixture.

7. Cover the pan with foil.

8. Chill in the refrigerator for 8 hours.

9. Preheat your grill.

10. Grease the grill with oil.

11. Cook the steak on the grill for 5 to 7 minutes per side.

Nutrients per Serving:

- Calories: 388.3
- Fat: 27.8 g
- Saturated Fat: 6.3 g
- Carbohydrates: 9.7 g
- Fiber: 0.1 g
- Protein: 24.8 g
- Cholesterol: 46.5 mg
- Sugars: 8.9 g
- Sodium: 663.1 mg
- Potassium: 407.7 mg

Swiss Steak

This Swiss steak recipe takes long hours of cooking, but the active prep time required is only a few minutes. Once you have got a taste of the amazing dish, you'll know that the long wait is surely worth it.

Serving Size: 6

Preparation Cooking Time: 10 hours and 30 minutes

Ingredients:

- Salt and pepper to taste
- ¼ cup flour
- 1 ½ lb. beef round
- 3 tablespoons soybean oil
- 1 onion, sliced
- 3 carrots, sliced
- 3 stalks celery, chopped
- 1 tablespoon Worcestershire sauce
- 28 oz. canned tomatoes, juice undrained
- 2 tablespoons brown sugar

Instructions:

1. Combine the salt, pepper and flour.

2. Coat the round steak with this mixture.

3. Next, pour the oil into a pan over medium heat.

4. Cook the onion, carrots and celery for 5 minutes, stirring often.

5. Stir in the steak and cook until brown on both sides.

6. Transfer the steak and veggies to your slow cooker.

7. Pour in the Worcestershire sauce and canned tomatoes with juice.

8. Stir in the sugar.

9. Cover the pot.

10. Cook on low setting for 10 hours.

Nutrients per Serving:

- Calories: 246.4
- Fat: 10.6 g
- Saturated Fat: 2.4 g
- Carbohydrates: 19.2 g
- Fiber: 2.9 g
- Protein: 16.8 g
- Cholesterol: 38.6 mg
- Sugars: 10.8 g
- Sodium: 314.9 mg
- Potassium: 604.9 mg

Grilled Rib Eye Steak

There's no need to spend a lot in the steakhouse when you can make rib eye steak as delicious as this at home without having to spend the whole day in the kitchen.

Serving Size: 4

Preparation Cooking Time: 3 hours and 35 minutes

Ingredients:

- ½ onion, minced
- ¼ cup garlic, crushed and minced
- ½ cup olive oil
- 6 tablespoons soy sauce
- 3 tablespoons steak seasoning
- 3 tablespoons steak sauce
- ¼ cup Worcestershire sauce
- 1 tablespoon fresh rosemary, chopped
- Salt and pepper to taste
- 4 rib eye steaks

Instructions:

1. Add the onion, garlic, olive oil, soy sauce, steak seasoning, steak sauce, Worcestershire sauce, rosemary, salt and pepper to a food processor.

2. Pulse until smooth.

3. Pierce the steaks using a fork.

4. Place in a shallow pan.

5. Next, pour the mixture on top of your steaks.

6. Coat the steaks with the mixture.

7. Cover and marinate in the refrigerator for 3 hours.

8. Preheat your grill.

9. Lastly, grill the steaks for 8 to 10 minutes per side.

Nutrients per Serving:

- Calories: 675.6
- Fat: 53.6 g
- Saturated Fat: 14.4 g
- Carbohydrates: 14.8 g
- Fiber: 1.6 g
- Protein: 33.7 g
- Cholesterol: 100.5 mg
- Sugars: 3.1 g
- Sodium: 7322.3 mg
- Potassium: 793.8 mg

Mojo Steak

Mojo is a Cuban sauce made with orange juice, garlic, herbs and spices. It lends incredible flavors to steak, making your dinner extra special.

Serving Size: 4

Preparation Cooking Time: 3 hours and 20 minutes

Ingredients:

- 2 lb. skirt steak, sliced into strips
- ¼ cup olive oil
- 6 cloves garlic, minced
- 5 tablespoons orange juice
- 2 tablespoons lime juice
- ½ teaspoon ground oregano
- 1 ½ teaspoons ground cumin
- Pinch cayenne pepper
- Salt and pepper to taste
- 1 onion, sliced
- 1 tablespoon olive oil
- 1 tablespoon lime juice
- ½ cup cilantro, chopped

Instructions:

1. Add the steaks to a shallow pan.

2. In a bowl, mix the lime juice, orange juice, olive oil, garlic, ground oregano, ground cumin, cayenne pepper, salt and pepper.

3. Pour the marinade into the pan.

4. Coat the steaks with the mixture.

5. Stir in the onion.

6. Cover and refrigerate for 3 hours.

7. Preheat your grill.

8. Then, grill the steaks for 3 minutes per side.

9. Drizzle with 1 tablespoon olive oil and 1 tablespoon lime juice.

10. Serve with the cilantro.

Nutrients per Serving:

- Calories: 381.5
- Fat: 23.2 g
- Saturated Fat: 5.7 g
- Carbohydrates: 16 g
- Fiber: 3.6 g
- Protein: 29.1 g
- Cholesterol: 50.6 mg
- Sugars: 6.5 g
- Sodium: 2116.6 mg
- Potassium: 576.2 mg

Beer Steaks

Beer is typically used for marinating steaks. In this recipe, we also add into the mix teriyaki sauce, garlic powder and brown sugar to infuse the steaks with deep sweet and savory flavors.

Serving Size: 4

Preparation Cooking Time: 1 hour and 20 minutes

Ingredients:

- 2 beef sirloin steaks
- ½ teaspoon garlic powder
- Salt and pepper to taste
- 2 tablespoons brown sugar
- 2 tablespoons teriyaki sauce
- ¼ cup beer

Instructions:

1. Preheat your grill.

2. Pierce the steaks with a fork.

3. Next, sprinkle both sides of the steaks with the garlic powder, salt and pepper.

4. In a bowl, combine the brown sugar, teriyaki sauce and beer.

5. Take 5 tablespoons of the mixture and use this to marinate the steaks for 30 minutes.

6. Reserve the rest of the sauce.

7. Grill the steaks approximately for 6 to 7 minutes per side.

8. Add the reserved sauce to a pan over medium heat.

9. Bring to a boil. Then, simmer for 10 minutes.

10. Pour the sauce over the grilled steaks and serve.

Nutrients per Serving:

- Calories: 389.7
- Fat: 20.8 g
- Saturated Fat: 8.3 g
- Carbohydrates: 9.2 g
- Fiber: 0.1 g
- Protein: 38.1 g
- Sugars: 7.9 g
- Cholesterol: 121.1 mg
- Sodium: 546.9 mg
- Potassium: 531.6 mg

Country-Style Steak

Also called smothered steak, country-style steak is the go-to recipe if you want a steak recipe that's not only undoubtedly easy to make but also filling and satisfying. Steak strips smothered in creamy gravy sauce and served with mashed potatoes.

Serving Size: 4

Preparation Cooking Time: 2 hours and 40 minutes

Ingredients:

- 1 cup all-purpose flour
- ¼ teaspoon garlic powder
- Salt and pepper to taste
- 1 lb. beef sirloin, sliced into strips
- ½ cup olive oil
- 2 cups beef broth
- Mashed potatoes

Instructions:

1. Preheat your oven to 350 degrees F.

2. Combine the garlic powder, flour, salt and pepper in a bowl.

3. Reserve 3 tablespoons of this mixture.

4. Dredge the beef strips in the remaining flour mixture.

5. Pour the olive oil into a pan over medium heat.

6. Fry the beef for 5 minutes per side.

7. Transfer browned beef into a baking pan.

8. In a bowl, combine the reserved flour mixture and broth.

9. Pour the broth on top of the steaks.

10. Cover the baking pan with foil.

11. Bake in the oven for 2 hours.

Nutrients per Serving:

- Calories: 355
- Fat: 19.9 g
- Saturated Fat: 4.0 g
- Carbohydrates: 24.6 g
- Fiber: 1 g
- Protein: 18.3 g
- Cholesterol: 27 mg
- Sugars: 0 g
- Sodium: 656 mg
- Potassium: 307 mg

Slow-Cooked London Broil

London broil is indeed a cut of beef that's ideal for slow cooking. In this recipe, we slow cook the meat in mushroom soup flavored with garlic and herbs.

Serving Size: 5

Preparation Cooking Time: 7 hours and 10 minutes

Ingredients:

- 1 ½ lb. beef round
- 2 cloves garlic, minced
- 10 oz. cream of mushrooms
- ½ cup water
- ½ teaspoon dried oregano
- ½ teaspoon dried basil leaves
- Salt to taste

Instructions:

1. First, combine all the ingredients in a slow cooker.

2. Stir.

3. Cover the pot.

4. Cook on low for 7 hours.

Nutrients per Serving:

- Calories: 219.6
- Fat: 8.1 g
- Saturated Fat: 2.4 g
- Carbohydrates: 4.6 g
- Fiber: 0.1 g
- Protein: 30.2 g
- Cholesterol: 72.5 mg
- Sugars: 0.9 g
- Sodium: 663.2 mg
- Potassium: 317.9 mg

Slow Cooked Round Steak

Enjoy succulent steak strips smothered with gravy with this simple and easy recipe.

Serving Size: 6

Preparation Cooking Time: 10 hours and 20 minutes

Ingredients:

- 3 potatoes
- 1 onion, sliced into rings
- 6 baby carrots, sliced
- 2 lb. beef round, sliced into strips
- ¾ cup water
- 10 oz. cream of mushroom soup
- 1 pack onion soup mix

Instructions:

1. Add the onion, potatoes and carrots in your slow cooker.

2. Arrange the beef on top.

3. In a bowl, mix the water, mushroom soup and onion soup mix.

4. Next, pour this mixture over the beef and veggies.

5. Seal the pot.

6. Cook on low for 10 hours.

Nutrients per Serving:

- Calories: 392.6
- Fat: 13.6 g
- Saturated Fat: 4.6 g
- Carbohydrates: 33.1 g
- Fiber: 4.5 g
- Protein: 33.8 g
- Cholesterol: 80.5 mg
- Sugars: 5 g
- Sodium: 828.6 mg
- Potassium: 824 mg

Filet Mignon with Mustard Sauce

A mouthwatering combination of savory flavors—this filet mignon smothered with mustard rosemary sauce. This pairs well with garlic mashed potatoes and steamed green beans.

Serving Size: 4

Preparation Cooking Time: 50 minutes

Ingredients:

- 4 beef tenderloins
- Salt and pepper to taste
- ¼ cup olive oil
- ¼ cup balsamic vinegar
- 1 tablespoon Dijon mustard
- 2 teaspoons dried rosemary
- 1 tablespoon butter
- 2 cups onions, sliced
- 1 teaspoon granulated sugar
- 4 oz. blue cheese

Instructions:

1. First, sprinkle the steaks with the salt and pepper.

2. Arrange the steaks in the baking pan.

3. Mix the olive oil, mustard, rosemary and balsamic vinegar in a bowl.

4. Pour this mixture into the baking pan.

5. Coat the steaks with the mixture.

6. Cover and marinate for 30 minutes.

7. While waiting, add the butter to a pan over medium heat.

8. Add the onion and cook for 2 minutes.

9. Stir in the sugar.

10. Cook until the onions have caramelized.

11. Preheat your grill.

12. Grill the steaks approximately for 5 to 7 minutes per side.

13. Top the steaks with the blue cheese and onions.

14. Lastly, grill for another 2 minutes or until the cheese has melted.

Nutrients per Serving:

- Calories: 590.1
- Fat: 43.4 g
- Saturated Fat: 16.3 g
- Carbohydrates: 13.4 g
- Fiber: 1.8 g
- Protein: 35.3 g
- Cholesterol: 124.5 mg
- Sugars: 6.9 g
- Sodium: 689.4 mg
- Potassium: 571.4 mg

Rib Eye Steak with Ginger Soy

Coat your rib eye steaks with a mix of ginger, soy, maple syrup, mustard and hot pepper sauce before cooking them on the grill.

Serving Size: 4

Preparation Cooking Time: 1 hour and 20 minutes

Ingredients:

- ¼ cup maple syrup
- ½ cup soy sauce
- 1 tablespoon ginger, minced
- ½ teaspoon hot pepper sauce
- 6 cloves garlic, minced
- 1 teaspoon sesame oil
- 1 teaspoon mustard powder
- ½ cup beer
- 4 rib eye steaks

Instructions:

1. Mix the maple syrup, soy sauce, ginger, hot pepper sauce, garlic, sesame oil, mustard powder and beer in a bowl.

2. Score both sides of the steaks with a knife.

3. Add the steaks to the mixture.

4. Turn to coat evenly.

5. Cover with foil.

6. Marinate inside the refrigerator for 1 hour.

7. Preheat your grill.

8. Add the steaks to the grill.

9. Increase heat to high.

10. Sear the steaks for 15 seconds per side.

11. Reduce heat and grill for 5 minutes per side.

12. Let rest before serving.

Nutrients per Serving:

- Calories: 466.9
- Fat: 27.1 g
- Saturated Fat: 10.7 g
- Carbohydrates: 18.8 g
- Fiber: 0.5 g
- Protein: 33.6 g
- Cholesterol: 100.5 mg
- Sugars: 12.4 g
- Sodium: 1894 mg
- Potassium: 576.3 mg

Ginger Steak

Ginger adds a strong zing to regular steak. It's nothing like you've ever tasted before.

Serving Size: 4

Preparation Cooking Time: 30 minutes

Ingredients:

- 4 beef sirloin steaks
- 2 tablespoons soy sauce
- 1 teaspoon ground ginger
- Salt and pepper to taste
- 1 teaspoon dried basil leaves
- 1 tablespoon mustard
- 1 teaspoon freshly squeezed lemon juice

Instructions:

1. Preheat the broiler in your oven.

2. Add the steaks to a broiling pan.

3. In a bowl, combine the remaining ingredients.

4. Pour the mixture over the steaks.

5. Turn to coat evenly.

6. Broil the steaks in the oven for 3 to 4 minutes per side.

Nutrients per Serving:

- Calories: 296.1
- Fat: 13.2 g
- Saturated Fat: 5.1 g
- Carbohydrates: 1.7 g
- Fiber: 0.5 g
- Protein: 40.3 g
- Cholesterol: 98.3 mg
- Sugars: 0.2 g
- Sodium: 868 mg
- Potassium: 540.6 mg

Caribbean Beef Loin

In this recipe, we drench beef loin with a Caribbean inspired sauce made with garlic powder, cinnamon, sage, oregano, rum, lemon juice and vinegar.

Serving Size: 6

Preparation Cooking Time: 3 hours

Ingredients:

- ½ teaspoon garlic powder
- 1/8 teaspoon ground cinnamon
- ¼ teaspoon ground sage
- ½ teaspoon ground oregano
- 1 tablespoon freshly squeezed lemon juice
- 1 oz. coconut rum
- ½ teaspoon vinegar
- Salt and pepper to taste
- 24 oz. beef sirloin, sliced into strips
- 4 slices onions, sliced
- 1 tablespoon olive oil

Instructions:

1. In a bowl, mix the garlic powder, ground herbs and spices, lemon juice, coconut rum, vinegar, salt and pepper.

2. Stir the steaks and onion into the mixture.

3. Cover and marinate for 2 hours and 30 minutes.

4. Add the oil to a pan over medium heat.

5. Cook the steaks approximately for 3 to 5 minutes per side.

Nutrients per Serving:

- Calories: 381
- Fat: 23.1 g
- Saturated Fat: 8.7 g
- Carbohydrates: 2.3 g
- Fiber: 0.3 g
- Protein: 37.3 g
- Cholesterol: 122.4 mg
- Sugars: 0.5 g
- Sodium: 183.9 mg
- Potassium: 518.6 mg

Salsa Steak

Top your steak with fresh tomato salsa for a fusion of incredible flavors you'd want to enjoy over and over.

Serving Size: 1

Preparation Cooking Time: 1 hour

Ingredients:

- 6 beef sirloins, sliced into strips
- Salt to taste
- 3 tablespoons water
- 1 cup salsa
- 1 potato, sliced into cubes
- 1 carrot
- 1 onion, sliced

Instructions:

1. Preheat your oven to 350 degrees F.

2. Next, season both sides of your steaks with the salt.

3. Line the baking pan with foil.

4. Add the water to the pan.

5. Add the steaks on top of a foil sheet.

6. Top with the salsa.

7. Cover with the foil.

8. Place the foil-covered steaks in the baking pan.

9. Bake in the oven for 1 hour.

Nutrients per Serving:

- Calories: 613.1
- Fat: 16.5 g
- Saturated Fat: 6.4 g
- Carbohydrates: 81.8 g
- Fiber: 11 g
- Protein: 38.2 g
- Cholesterol: 90.8 mg
- Sugars: 18.4 g
- Sodium: 2142.2 mg
- Potassium: 2419.5 mg

Peppercorn Steak

Here's a top-rated steak recipe that would make you feel like you're dining in a fancy restaurant—sirloin steak cooked in garlic butter sauce with wine, drenched with cream with brandy, and flavored with black peppercorns.

Serving Size: 4

Preparation Cooking Time: 45 minutes

Ingredients:

- 2 sirloin steaks
- 3 tablespoons black peppercorns
- Salt to taste
- 1 tablespoon lemon pepper
- 5 tablespoons butter
- 2 cloves garlic, minced
- ½ cup red wine
- 3 tablespoons brandy
- 1 shallot, minced
- ¼ cup green onions, chopped
- 1 cup cream
- 1 teaspoon sugar

Instructions:

1. First, press the peppercorns on both sides of the sirloin steaks.

2. Sprinkle with the salt and lemon pepper.

3. Next, add the butter to a pan over medium high heat.

4. Cook the garlic for 30 seconds, stirring frequently.

5. Pour in the wine. Then, simmer for 1 minute.

6. Place the steaks in the pan.

7. Cook for 5 minutes per side.

8. Reduce heat to low.

9. Next, add the brandy to the pan along with the shallots and green onion.

10. Pour in the cream and stir in the sugar.

11. Cook for 1 minute.

12. Lastly, pour the sauce over the steaks and serve.

Nutrients per Serving:

- Calories: 490
- Fat: 35.8 g
- Saturated Fat: 20.1 g
- Protein: 20.3 g
- Carbohydrates: 9.1 g
- Fiber: 1.6 g
- Cholesterol: 138.5 mg
- Sugars: 2 g
- Sodium: 1089.1 mg
- Potassium: 436.5 mg

Steak Strips in Mushroom Sauce

Smothering your steak strips in creamy mushroom sauce is definitely a great way to add pizzazz to a regular dinner at home. This recipe is quick and straightforward, but gives you stellar results.

Serving Size: 6

Preparation Cooking Time: 50 minutes

Ingredients:

- 2 ½ lb. beef, sliced into strips
- Salt and pepper to taste
- ¼ cup butter
- 1 shallot, chopped
- 4 Portobello mushrooms, sliced
- ½ bottle red wine
- 28 oz. beef broth
- 2 cloves garlic, minced
- ½ teaspoon dried thyme
- 1 cup cream

Instructions:

1. First, preheat your grill.

2. Second, season the steak strips with salt and pepper.

3. Grill for 2 to 3 minutes per side.

4. Next, add the butter to a pan over medium high heat.

5. Cook the shallots for 1 minute, stirring often.

6. Add the mushrooms. Then, cook for 5 minutes.

7. Next, pour in the wine and broth to deglaze the pan.

8. Increase heat.

9. Bring to a boil.

10. Reduce and simmer until reduced by half.

11. Add the garlic, thyme and cream.

12. Turn off the heat.

13. Pour the mushroom sauce over the steaks.

Nutrients per Serving:

- Calories: 454.6
- Fat: 25.4 g
- Saturated Fat: 11.9 g
- Carbohydrates: 9.3 g
- Fiber: 1.3 g
- Protein: 35.2 g
- Cholesterol: 121.2 mg
- Sugars: 2.1 g
- Sodium: 672 mg
- Potassium: 944.5 mg

Barbecue Buttered Steaks

Here's a superb recipe that drenches succulent steak in barbecue butter sauce. This is a quick steak recipe that can be prepared in less than 10 minutes.

Serving Size: 2

Preparation Cooking Time: 8 minutes

Ingredients:

- 2 sirloin steaks
- Salt and pepper to taste
- 1 tablespoon butter
- 1 ½ tablespoons barbecue sauce
- ½ cup beef broth
- 1 tablespoon vegetable oil
- Hot pepper sauce

Instructions:

1. First, flatten the steaks with a meat mallet.

2. Second, season both sides of the steaks with the salt and pepper.

3. In a bowl, mix the butter, barbecue sauce and broth.

4. Season the sauce with pepper.

5. Next, pour the oil into a pan over high heat.

6. Wait for it to smoke.

7. Add the steaks and sear for 45 seconds per side.

8. Transfer the steaks to a plate.

9. Add the butter mixture to the pan.

10. Reduce heat to medium.

11. Bring to a boil.

12. Scrape the browned bits using a wooden spoon.

13. Simmer for 5 minutes.

14. Pour the barbecue butter mixture over the steaks and serve.

Nutrients per Serving:

- Calories: 318
- Fat: 22 g
- Saturated Fat: 8.0 g
- Carbohydrates: 4.6 g
- Fiber: 0.2 g
- Protein: 24.1 g
- Cholesterol: 81 mg
- Sugars: 3 g
- Sodium: 409 mg
- Potassium: 372 mg

Irish Steaks

Any steak lovers will be thrilled to have a taste of this Irish steak, flavored not only with butter, garlic and herbs but also with Irish whiskey.

Serving Size: 4

Preparation Cooking Time: 30 minutes

Ingredients:

- 2 tablespoons soybean oil
- 3 tablespoons butter
- 1 onion, sliced
- 4 sirloin beef steaks
- 1 clove garlic, minced
- ¼ cup Irish whiskey
- 2 tablespoons parsley, chopped
- Salt and pepper to taste

Instructions:

1. First, add the oil and butter to a pan over medium heat.

2. Let the butter melt.

3. Add the onions. Then, cook for 10 minutes, stirring frequently.

4. Push the onions to one side of your pan.

5. Rub the sirloin steaks with the minced garlic.

6. Add the steaks to the pan.

7. Cook for 3 minutes per side.

8. Remove the pan from the stove.

9. Pour the whiskey into the pan carefully.

10. Stir in the onions, steaks and sauce.

11. Simmer over medium low heat.

12. Add the parsley, salt and pepper to the sauce.

13. Drizzle the steaks with the sauce before serving.

Nutrients per Serving:

- Calories: 362.7
- Fat: 25 g
- Saturated Fat: 10.3 g
- Carbohydrates: 5.7 g
- Fiber: 1 g
- Protein: 19.7 g
- Cholesterol: 83.2 mg
- Sugars: 2.5 g
- Sodium: 107 mg
- Potassium: 348.3 mg

Steak in Marsala Sauce

Marsala sauce is used to flavor up sirloin steak in this quick and easy recipe. Marsala sauce is typically made with onion, garlic, mushrooms, herbs, butter, cream and Marsala wine, thus the name. It is sometimes used for deglazing or sometimes adding last to the dish before serving.

Serving Size: 4

Preparation Cooking Time: 30 minutes

Ingredients:

- 1 lb. beef sirloin, fat trimmed and sliced
- Cooking spray
- 1 cup onions, sliced
- 2 cloves garlic, minced
- 1 cup mushrooms
- 2 tablespoons parsley, chopped
- ¼ cup water
- ⅓ cup Marsala wine
- ¼ cup beef stock
- 1 cup cream
- Pepper to taste

Instructions:

1. Preheat your broiler.

2. Add the steak to a broiler pan.

3. Next, broil in the oven for 5 minutes per side.

4. While waiting, prepare the sauce.

5. Spray a pan with oil.

6. Place the pan over medium heat.

7. Cook the onion, garlic and mushrooms for 3 minutes, stirring often.

8. Add the parsley, water, wine and beef broth.

9. Season with the pepper.

10. Next, bring to a boil.

11. Reduce heat. Then, simmer approximately for 5 minutes or until sauce is reduced.

12. Pour the sauce over the steak and serve.

Nutrients per Serving:

- Calories: 339.2
- Fat: 17.6 g
- Saturated Fat: 7 g
- Carbohydrates: 5.6 g
- Fiber: 0.7 g
- Protein: 32.5 g
- Cholesterol: 102.2 mg
- Sugars: 2.8 g
- Sodium: 77.6 mg
- Potassium: 534.2 mg

Steak with Mushroom Tarragon

Serve your steaks with shiitake mushrooms, drizzled with sauce made with butter, shallots, white wine and tarragon.

Serving Size: 2

Preparation Cooking Time: 30 minutes

Ingredients:

- 12 oz. beef top sirloin
- Salt and pepper to taste
- 2 tablespoons vegetable oil
- ½ shallots, chopped
- 1 clove garlic, minced
- ⅓ cup Shiitake mushrooms, sliced
- ¼ cup butter
- ¼ cup red wine
- ½ cup reduced-sodium beef broth
- 2 tablespoons fresh tarragon, chopped

Instructions:

1. First, sprinkle both sides of the steak with the salt and pepper.

2. Add the oil to a pan over high heat.

3. Once hot, cook the steak for 3 to 4 minutes per side.

4. Transfer the steak to a plate.

5. Keep warm by tenting with foil.

6. Remove the oil in the pan.

7. Wipe dry with a paper towel.

8. Reduce heat to medium low. Then, cook the shallots, garlic and mushrooms.

9. Next, add the wine and cook for 5 minutes.

10. Add the broth.

11. Reduce heat.

12. Stir in the butter and tarragon.

13. Sprinkle with a little salt and pepper.

14. Lastly, pour the sauce over the steak before serving.

Nutrients per Serving:

- Calories: 568.6
- Fat: 42.6 g
- Saturated Fat: 19 g
- Carbohydrates: 5.5 g
- Fiber: 0.4 g
- Protein: 32.6 g
- Cholesterol: 119.3 mg
- Sugars: 1.1 g
- Sodium: 446.6 mg
- Potassium: 527.9 mg

Adobo Steak

Marinate your beef sirloin in chipotle chili sauce and cook on the grill until brown on the outside yet tender and juicy inside.

Serving Size: 4

Preparation Cooking Time: 2 hours and 30 minutes

Ingredients:

- 1 tablespoon garlic, minced
- 1 tablespoon lime juice
- 1 teaspoon ground cumin
- 1 teaspoon ground oregano
- 2 tablespoons chipotle peppers in adobo sauce, sauce undrained
- 8 oz. beef sirloin, sliced
- Salt to taste

Instructions:

1. Combine the garlic, lime juice, cumin and oregano in a bowl.

2. Add the chipotle peppers and 1 tablespoon of its adobo sauce.

3. Pierce the beef with a fork.

4. Season with the salt and pepper.

5. Add the chipotle sauce mixture over the steaks.

6. Turn to coat evenly.

7. Cover with foil.

8. Marinate in the refrigerator for 2 hours.

9. Preheat your grill.

10. Grease the grill grate with oil.

11. Add the steaks to the grill.

12. Cook approximately for 5 to 6 minutes per side.

Nutrients per Serving:

- Calories: 342.3
- Fat: 18.8 g
- Saturated Fat: 7.4 g
- Carbohydrates: 3.7 g
- Fiber: 1.1 g
- Protein: 37.6 g
- Cholesterol: 119.5 mg
- Sugars: 0.3 g
- Sodium: 428.6 mg
- Potassium: 531.3 mg

Korean Steak

Make it seem like you've taken a trip to Korea by preparing this awesome Korean steak dish at home.

Serving Size: 6

Preparation Cooking Time: 12 hours and 30 minutes

Ingredients:

- 2 lb. chuck roast, sliced
- ½ cup soy sauce
- 2 tablespoons sesame oil
- 2 cloves garlic, minced
- 3 shallots, chopped
- 5 tablespoons mirin
- 5 tablespoons granulated sugar
- 2 tablespoons white sesame seeds, divided

Instructions:

1. Add the beef to a bowl.

2. In another bowl, combine the entire ingredients, reserving half of the sesame seeds for garnishing later.

3. Pour the mixture into the bowl with beef.

4. Turn to coat.

5. Cover the bowl.

6. Refrigerate for 12 hours.

7. Place your pan over medium heat.

8. Cook the beef approximately for 5 to 7 minutes per side.

9. Garnish with white sesame seeds.

Nutrients per Serving:

- Calories: 376.3
- Fat: 21.9 g
- Saturated Fat: 7.1 g
- Carbohydrates: 21.4 g
- Fiber: 0.8 g
- Protein: 20.6 g
- Cholesterol: 68.8 mg
- Sugars: 15.5 g
- Sodium: 1249.1 mg
- Potassium: 306.4 mg

Flank Steak Rolls

This isn't like any other steaks you've tried before. This one is made with layers of spinach, feta and onion, and rolled up before serving. It's unique, delicious and easy to make all at the same time.

Serving Size: 6

Preparation Cooking Time: 9 hours and 30 minutes

Ingredients:

- ¼ cup olive oil
- 1 tablespoon lemon juice
- 2 cloves garlic, minced and divided
- ¼ cup red wine
- ¼ cup soy sauce
- 1 tablespoon Dijon mustard
- ¼ cup Worcestershire sauce
- ½ teaspoon pepper
- 1 teaspoon Italian seasoning
- 1 ½ lb. flank steak
- ¼ cup onion, sliced
- ½ cup feta cheese
- 1 cup spinach, chopped
- ¼ cup breadcrumbs

Instructions:

1. First, in a bowl, combine the olive oil, lemon juice, half of garlic, red wine, soy sauce, Dijon mustard, Worcestershire sauce, pepper and Italian seasoning.

2. Add the steak to the bowl.

3. Cover and refrigerate for 8 hours.

4. Preheat your oven to 350 degrees F.

5. Next, mash the garlic and salt until it turns to paste.

6. Spread the garlic paste on the steak.

7. Add the onion, feta cheese, spinach and breadcrumbs on top of the steak.

8. Next, roll them up and secure with a toothpick.

9. Add the steak roll to a baking pan.

10. Bake for 1 hour.

11. Let sit for 5 minutes before slicing.

Nutrients per Serving:

- Calories: 299.6
- Fat: 20.2 g
- Saturated Fat: 6.6 g
- Carbohydrates: 10.1 g
- Fiber: 1.3 g
- Protein: 17.5 g
- Cholesterol: 46.8 mg
- Sugars: 2.7 g
- Sodium: 1099.2 mg
- Potassium: 423.3 mg

New York Steak

Make juicy, tender and flavorful steak on the grill using this fuss-free recipe.

Serving Size: 4

Preparation Cooking Time: 2 hours and 30 minutes

Ingredients:

- ½ cup olive oil
- ½ cup Worcestershire sauce
- ¼ cup garlic, minced
- ¼ cup Montreal steak seasoning
- ½ teaspoon dried basil leaves
- ½ teaspoon Italian seasoning
- 1 tablespoon red wine vinegar
- 4 New York strip steaks

Instructions:

1. Combine the olive oil, garlic, red wine vinegar, Montreal steak seasoning, Worcestershire sauce, Italian seasoning and dried basil leaves in a bowl.

2. Add this mixture to a bowl.

3. Pierce the steaks using a fork.

4. Coat the steaks with this mixture.

5. Cover the bowl.

6. Marinate in the refrigerator for 2 hours.

7. Preheat your grill.

8. Grease the grill grate.

9. Cook the steaks approximately for 3 to 4 minutes per side.

Nutrients per Serving:

- Calories: 585.9
- Fat: 41 g
- Saturated Fat: 8.8 g
- Carbohydrates: 12.9 g
- Fiber: 0.6 g
- Protein: 39.4 g
- Cholesterol: 102.3 mg
- Sugars: 3.5 g
- Sodium: 224 mg
- Potassium: 911.7 mg

Bacon-Wrapped Filet Mignon with Peppercorn Sauce

Perfectly tender filet mignon drenched in peppercorn sauce—you'll love this sophisticated by the easy to follow recipe that gives you a five-star steak dish.

Serving Size: 4

Preparation Cooking Time: 1 hour and 30 minutes

Ingredients:

Peppercorn Sauce

- 1 ¼ cups beef broth
- 1 teaspoon black peppercorns
- 1 oz. whiskey
- 1 cup cream

Steaks

- 4 beef tenderloin steaks
- 4 slices bacon
- Salt to taste
- 1 tablespoon olive oil
- 1 teaspoon shallots, chopped
- 1 cup mushrooms
- 1 clove garlic, minced
- 1 oz. whiskey
- 1 teaspoon Dijon mustard

Instructions:

1. First, in a pan over medium heat, add the broth and peppercorns.

2. Simmer until the broth has been reduced to 1 cup.

3. Pour in the whiskey and cream.

4. Simmer for 5 minutes.

5. Transfer to a bowl and set aside.

6. Season the steaks with salt.

7. Wrap each steak with the bacon.

8. Next, pour the olive oil into a pan over medium heat.

9. Cook the shallot, mushrooms and garlic for 1 to 2 minutes, stirring often.

10. Transfer to a plate and set aside.

11. Add the steaks to the pan.

12. Next, cook for 3 to 5 minutes per side.

13. Transfer to another plate.

14. Pour the whiskey to the pan to deglaze.

15. Pour in the peppercorn sauce, mushroom mixture and mustard.

16. Simmer until sauce has thickened.

17. Pour the sauce over the steaks wrapped with bacon and serve.

Nutrients per Serving:

- Calories: 748.4
- Fat: 57.3 g
- Saturated Fat: 24.6 g
- Carbohydrates: 6.7 g
- Fiber: 1 g
- Protein: 41.4 g
- Cholesterol: 215.4 mg
- Sugars: 0.4 g
- Sodium: 1175.4 mg
- Potassium: 705.8 mg

Steak Sauerbraten

Sauerbraten is a traditional German marinated meat dish that's popular all over the world. It can be made using beef, lamb, pork, horse or lamb. In this steak sauerbraten recipe, we make it using round steak.

Serving Size: 4

Preparation Cooking Time: 1 hour and 20 minutes

Ingredients:

- 1 tablespoon vegetable oil
- 1 ½ lb. round steak, sliced into strips
- 1 packet brown gravy
- 2 cups water
- 1 tablespoon onion powder
- 1 teaspoon Worcestershire sauce
- 2 tablespoons cider vinegar
- 1 bay leaf, crumbled
- 1 tablespoon brown sugar
- ¼ teaspoon ground ginger
- Salt and pepper to taste

Instructions:

1. Pour the oil into your pan over medium heat.

2. Cook the steak strips for 3 to 5 minutes per side.

3. Transfer to a plate.

4. Pour the water and gravy powder into the pan.

5. Bring to a boil, stirring frequently.

6. Reduce heat and stir in the rest of the ingredients.

7. Put the steak strips back to the pan.

8. Reduce heat and simmer for 1 hour.

9. Discard the bay leaf before serving.

Nutrients per Serving:

- Calories: 568.6
- Fat: 42.6 g
- Saturated Fat: 19 g
- Carbohydrates: 5.5 g
- Fiber: 0.4 g
- Protein: 32.6 g
- Cholesterol: 119.3mg
- Sugars: 1.1 g
- Sodium: 446.6 mg
- Potassium: 527.9 mg

Steak with Red Wine Sauce

If you actually want to make a special dinner at home, you can't go wrong with this simple but satisfying steak with red wine sauce recipe.

Serving Size: 6

Preparation Cooking Time: 45 minutes

Ingredients:

- 1 tablespoon soybean oil
- 8 oz. mushrooms, sliced
- 2 red onions, sliced
- 1 tablespoon soybean oil
- 6 New York strip steaks
- Salt to taste
- 1 cup red wine
- 2 tablespoons Dijon mustard
- 1 cup beef broth
- 1 cup cream

Instructions:

1. First, add 1 tablespoon vegetable oil to a pan over medium high heat.

2. Cook the mushrooms and onions for 10 minutes, stirring frequently.

3. Dry the steaks with paper towels.

4. Next, sprinkle both sides with the salt and pepper.

5. Add the steaks to the pan.

6. Cook for 5 to 6 minutes per side.

7. Pour the wine into the pan.

8. Stir in the mustard and beef broth.

9. Add the cream.

10. Simmer for 5 minutes.

11. Place the steaks on a serving plate.

12. Top with the onions and mushrooms.

13. Lastly, pour the sauce over the steaks and serve.

Nutrients per Serving:

- Calories: 649.1
- Fat: 33.9 g
- Saturated Fat: 15.4 g
- Carbohydrates: 7.5 g
- Fiber: 1 g
- Protein: 69.3 g
- Cholesterol: 199.6 mg
- Sugars: 2.2 g
- Sodium: 413 mg
- Potassium: 1107.4 mg

Bourbon Strip Steak

Grilled steak made even more flavorful with bourbon—a dish that's bound to impress family and friends.

Serving Size: 2

Preparation Cooking Time: 1 hour and 40 minutes

Ingredients:

- 3 cups bourbon whiskey
- 2 strip steaks
- 1 cup brown sugar

Instructions:

1. Flatten the meat using a meat mallet.

2. Score the steaks but do not slice all the way through.

3. Place these in a baking pan.

4. Pour the bourbon over the steaks.

5. Sprinkle the brown sugar on each side.

6. Next, cover and marinate in the refrigerator for 1 hour.

7. Preheat your grill.

8. Add the steaks on the grill.

9. Cook approximately for 4 to 5 minutes per side.

Nutrients per Serving:

- Calories: 1597.7
- Fat: 20.9 g
- Saturated Fat: 8.3 g
- Carbohydrates: 108.3 g
- Fiber: 0 g
- Protein: 25.4 g
- Cholesterol: 78.6 mg
- Sugars: 106.7 g
- Sodium: 97 mg
- Potassium: 497.6 mg

Chicago-Style Steak

Flavor up your strip steaks with herbs, spices and apricot jam in this easy-to-prepare recipe that you'd find yourself making more often.

Serving Size: 2

Preparation Cooking Time: 1 hour and 40 minutes

Ingredients:

- 1 tablespoon olive oil
- 2 tablespoons apricot jam
- 1 clove garlic, minced
- ½ teaspoon granulated sugar
- ½ teaspoon ground cinnamon
- 2 strip steaks
- Salt to taste

Instructions:

1. Combine the olive oil, apricot jam, garlic, sugar and ground cinnamon in a bowl.

2. Score the steaks on both sides.

3. Season with the salt and pepper.

4. Place the steaks in a baking pan.

5. Pour the apricot mixture over the steaks.

6. Turn to coat.

7. Cover with foil.

8. Marinate in the refrigerator for 1 hour.

9. Preheat your grill.

10. Add the steaks to the grill.

11. Grill for 5 minutes per side.

Nutrients per Serving:

- Calories: 439.2
- Fat: 19.3 g
- Saturated Fat: 5.7 g
- Carbohydrates: 14.9 g
- Fiber: 0.4 g
- Protein: 49.1 g
- Cholesterol: 133.9 mg
- Sugars: 9.7 g
- Sodium: 142.2 mg
- Potassium: 816.1 mg

Thyme Steaks with Mushrooms

Thyme adds a bit of minty flavor to steak while paprika gives it a zing. Serve this delicious grilled steak with roasted carrots or mashed potatoes with gravy.

Serving Size: 4

Preparation Cooking Time: 30 minutes

Ingredients:

- Salt and pepper to taste
- ½ teaspoon garlic powder
- ½ teaspoon dried thyme
- ½ teaspoon onion powder
- 2 teaspoons paprika
- 1 lb. beef short loin
- ¼ cup shallots, chopped
- 8 oz. mushrooms
- 2 tablespoons butter
- 2 tablespoons red wine
- 1 tablespoon soybean oil

Instructions:

1. In a bowl, combine the paprika, thyme, salt, onion powder, pepper, and garlic powder.

2. Season both sides of the steak with this mixture. Set aside.

3. Next, add the butter to a pan over medium high heat.

4. Cook the shallots and mushrooms for 3 minutes.

5. Pour in the red wine.

6. Reduce heat to medium.

7. Simmer until liquid has been reduced.

8. Transfer the mixture to a bowl.

9. Pour the oil into another pan over medium high heat.

10. Cook the steak for 5 minutes per side.

11. Top the steak with the mushrooms before serving.

Nutrients per Serving:

- Calories: 253.1
- Fat: 15.9 g
- Saturated Fat: 6.7 g
- Carbohydrates: 5.3 g
- Fiber: 1.3 g
- Protein: 21.6 g
- Cholesterol: 66.4 mg
- Sugars: 1.6 g
- Sodium: 673.2 mg
- Potassium: 529.8 mg

Koji Steak

Applying koji to steak does something incredible—its enzymes effectively tenderize the meat. Both the texture and taste resemble that of an aged steak. You can try this at home using this recipe.

Serving Size: 2

Preparation Cooking Time: 3 days and 30 minutes

Ingredients:

- ¾ cup koji rice
- 2 strip steaks
- Salt to taste
- 2 tablespoons butter

Instructions:

1. Add the rice to a food processor.

2. Grind until a little powdery.

3. Spread the koji rice on the strip steaks.

4. Place on a shallow pan.

5. Refrigerate without cover for 3 days.

6. When ready to cook, season the steaks with the salt.

7. Next, add the butter to a pan over medium high heat.

8. Sear the steaks for 2 minutes per side.

9. Reduce heat, then cook for another 5 minutes per side.

10. Let rest for 10 minutes before serving.

Nutrients per Serving:

- Calories: 888
- Fat: 38.1 g
- Saturated Fat: 15.0 g
- Carbohydrates: 54.9 g
- Fiber: 0.3 g
- Protein: 76.8 g
- Cholesterol: 164 mg
- Sugars: 0 g
- Sodium: 334 mg
- Potassium: 976 mg

Roasted Steak

Most steak recipes require frying or searing in a skillet. But in this recipe, we roast the strip steaks flavored with herbs and spices in the oven, and the result is truly incredible.

Serving Size: 4

Preparation Cooking Time: 40 minutes

Ingredients:

- 5 tablespoons olive oil, divided
- 1 teaspoon dried oregano
- 1 teaspoon ground cumin
- 1 teaspoon red pepper flakes
- 2 strip steaks

Instructions:

1. Add half of the olive oil to a bowl.

2. Stir in the oregano, cumin and red pepper flakes.

3. Pour the remaining oil into a pan over high heat.

4. Sear the steaks for 2 minutes per side.

5. Coat the steaks with the oregano mixture.

6. Wrap the steaks in foil.

7. Next, bake in your oven at 350 degrees F for 10 to 15 minutes.

8. Let rest for 3 minutes before slicing and serving.

Nutrients per Serving:

- Calories: 608
- Fat: 34.7 g
- Saturated Fat: 9.0 g
- Carbohydrates: 4.2 g
- Fiber: 1 g
- Protein: 66.4 g
- Cholesterol: 132 mg
- Sugars: 0 g
- Sodium: 1015 mg
- Potassium: 944 mg

Sweet Savory Steak

This melt-in-your-mouth steak dish is best served with roasted potatoes or fresh green salad.

Serving Size: 4

Preparation Cooking Time: 1 hour and 40 minutes

Ingredients:

- 4 rib eye steaks
- 2 cups soy sauce
- 1 cup ketchup
- 4 cloves garlic, minced
- 1 tablespoon brown sugar

Instructions:

1. Place the rib eye steaks in a baking pan.

2. Combine the rest of the ingredients in a bowl.

3. Next, pour the soy sauce mixture over your steaks.

4. Turn to coat.

5. Cover and marinate for 1 hour.

6. Preheat your grill.

7. Grill the steaks approximately for 5 to 7 minutes per side.

Nutrients per Serving:

- Calories: 292.8
- Fat: 15.7 g
- Saturated Fat: 6.4 g
- Carbohydrates: 10.7 g
- Fiber: 1.1 g
- Protein: 26.7 g
- Cholesterol: 60.3 mg
- Sugars: 2.2 g
- Sodium: 7262.9 mg
- Potassium: 546.3 mg

Rib Eye Steaks with Bell Peppers

This Mexican-inspired steak recipe is not only vibrant and colorful but also bursting with savory flavors.

Serving Size: 4

Preparation Cooking Time: 45 minutes

Ingredients:

- 1 tablespoon vegetable oil
- 4 rib eye steaks
- 1 green bell pepper, sliced
- 1 onion, sliced into wedges
- 4 cloves garlic, minced
- 1 red bell pepper, sliced
- 3 tablespoons Fajita seasoning
- 1 tablespoon lime juice
- 1 yellow bell pepper, sliced

Instructions:

1. First, pour the oil into a pan over medium high heat.

2. Sear the rib eye steaks for 2 minutes per side.

3. Transfer to a plate.

4. Next, add the onion, garlic, and bell peppers to the pan.

5. Cook for 5 minutes.

6. Drizzle the steaks with lime juice.

7. Reduce heat.

8. Cover and simmer for 1 hour.

Nutrients per Serving:

- Calories: 444.8
- Fat: 29.8 g
- Saturated Fat: 11.1 g
- Carbohydrates: 11.9 g
- Fiber: 2.1 g
- Protein: 32 g
- Cholesterol: 100.5 mg
- Sugars: 3.4 g
- Sodium: 397.4 mg
- Potassium: 611.6 mg

Italian Rib Eye

The combination of garlic, parsley, basil, oregano and rosemary intensifies the natural flavor of meat.

Serving Size: 3

Preparation Cooking Time: 1 hour and 40 minutes

Ingredients:

- 1 tablespoon basil, chopped
- 1 tablespoon oregano, chopped
- 1 teaspoon rosemary, chopped
- 1 tablespoon parsley, chopped
- 10 cloves garlic, minced
- Salt and pepper to taste
- ½ cup olive oil
- 2 tablespoons balsamic vinegar
- 3 rib eye steaks

Instructions:

1. Add the basil, oregano, rosemary, parsley, garlic, salt and pepper to a bowl.

2. Mash to turn it into a paste.

3. Pour in the olive oil and vinegar.

4. Blend well.

5. Spread half of this mixture on both sides of the steaks.

6. Cover and marinate for 1 hour.

7. Preheat your grill.

8. Grill the steaks approximately for 5 to 7 minutes per side.

Nutrients per Serving:

- Calories: 1077.8
- Fat: 93.9 g
- Saturated Fat: 28.5 g
- Carbohydrates: 5.7 g
- Fiber: 0.5 g
- Protein: 50.7 g
- Cholesterol: 187.6 mg
- Sugars: 1.6 g
- Sodium: 2082.7 mg
- Potassium: 942.8 mg

Grilled Steak with Strawberry Sauce

The strawberry reduction sauce turns ordinary grilled steak into something exquisite. You can also use cranberry juice in lieu of the wine when preparing this recipe.

Serving Size: 4

Preparation Cooking Time: 45 minutes

Ingredients:

- Cooking spray
- 4 beef top loin steaks
- Salt and pepper to taste
- 2 shallots, chopped
- ½ cup red wine
- 2 sprigs rosemary, chopped
- 2 teaspoons sugar
- 2 tablespoons balsamic vinegar
- 1 ½ cups strawberries, sliced

Instructions:

1. Spray your pan with oil.

2. Place the pan over medium heat.

3. Cook the shallots for 5 minutes, stirring often.

4. Turn off the heat.

5. Pour in the wine.

6. Add the rosemary.

7. Put the pan back to medium heat.

8. Cook for 3 minutes.

9. Add the sugar, vinegar and strawberries.

10. Cook for 4 minutes.

11. Discard the sprigs.

12. Preheat your grill.

13. Grill the steaks approximately for 5 to 6 minutes per side.

14. Pour the sauce over the steaks before serving.

Nutrients per Serving:

- Calories: 225
- Fat: 5 g
- Saturated fat: 2 g
- Carbohydrates: 17 g
- Fiber: 3 g
- Protein: 23 g
- Cholesterol: 59 mg
- Sugars: 10 g
- Sodium: 342 mg
- Potassium: 537 mg

Indian Steak

Infuse your steak with strong and intense flavors you can't get enough of using Indian spices. Serve Indian steak with grilled cauliflower and mango salad.

Serving Size: 4

Preparation Cooking Time: 30 minutes

Ingredients:

- 1 teaspoon ground coriander
- ⅛ teaspoon red pepper flakes
- ¼ teaspoon ground turmeric
- ¼ teaspoon ground ginger
- ½ teaspoon ground cumin
- ½ teaspoon garlic powder
- Salt and pepper to taste
- 1 lb. beef flank steak

Instructions:

1. Preheat your broiler.

2. Combine the coriander, ginger, cumin, garlic powder, red pepper flakes, turmeric, salt and pepper in a bowl.

3. Score the steak but do not slice all the way through.

4. Rub the mixture all over the steak.

5. Add the steak to a broiler pan.

6. Broil for 10 minutes per side.

Nutrients per Serving:

- Calories: 209
- Fat: 8.4 g
- Saturated fat: 3.4 g
- Carbohydrates: 8.1 g
- Fiber: 1.1 g
- Protein: 24.8 g
- Cholesterol: 74 mg
- Sugars: 6 g
- Sodium: 209 mg
- Potassium: 513 mg

Coffee Steaks

Rub your steaks with coffee, chili and herbs before cooking on the grill, and you get incredible tasting meat that you'd love to share with family and friends.

Serving Size: 4

Preparation Cooking Time: 40 minutes

Ingredients:

- 2 teaspoons coffee
- 2 teaspoons chili pepper
- 1 teaspoon mustard
- 1 teaspoon paprika
- 1 teaspoon dried oregano
- 1 teaspoon brown sugar
- ¼ teaspoon ground cumin
- Salt and pepper to taste
- 1 lb. sirloin steaks
- Cooking spray

Instructions:

1. In a bowl, mix the coffee, chili pepper, mustard, paprika, dried oregano, brown sugar, ground cumin, salt and pepper.

2. Spray the beef with oil.

3. Sprinkle both sides of the beef with this mixture.

4. Rub with your fingers.

5. Grill the beef for 4 to 6 minutes per side.

Nutrients per Serving:

- Calories: 292
- Fat: 9.3 g
- Saturated fat: 2.6 g
- Carbohydrates: 23.4 g
- Fiber: 5.4 g
- Protein: 28.4 g
- Cholesterol: 65 mg
- Sugars: 7 g
- Sodium: 552 mg
- Potassium: 845 mg

Garlic Rosemary Prime Rib

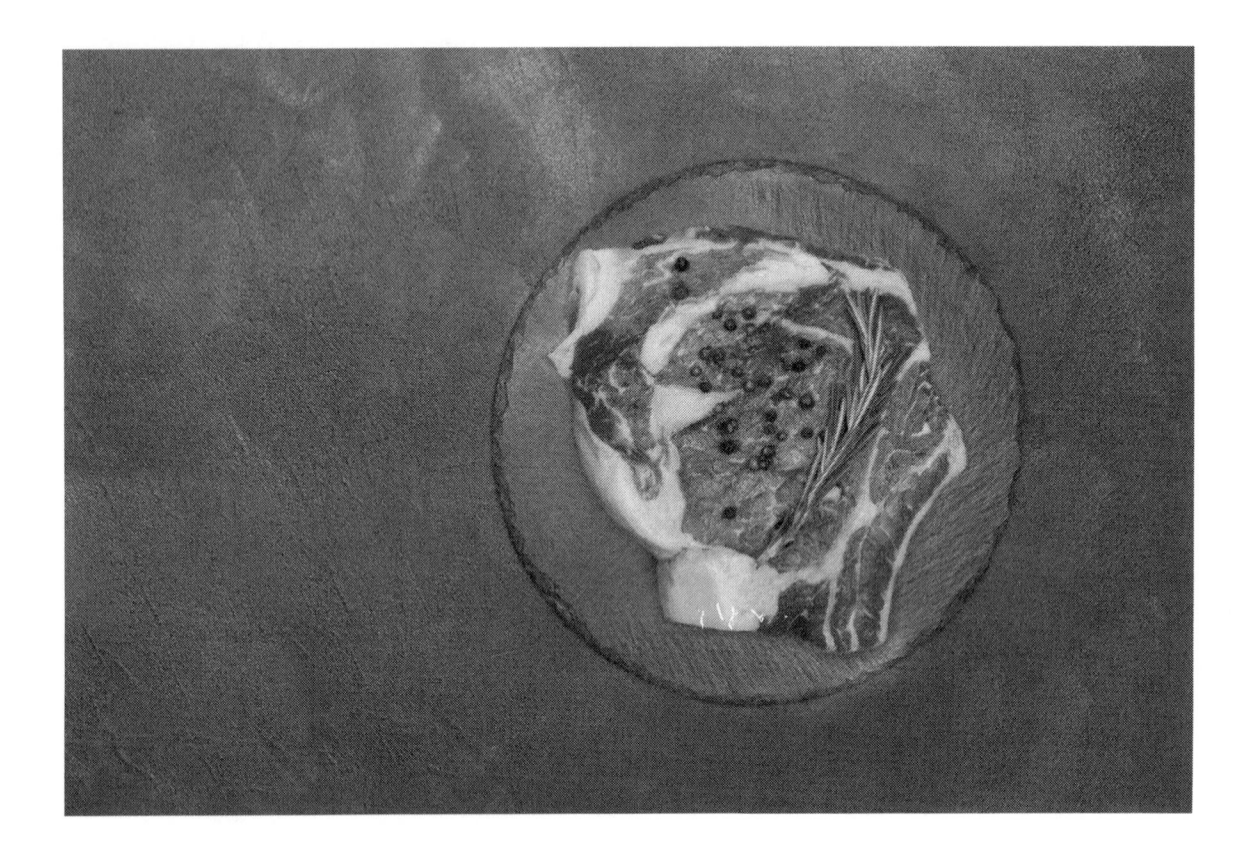

Rub your prime rib steaks with garlic and season with fresh rosemary before cooking in red wine sauce.

Serving Size: 8

Preparation Cooking Time: 1 hour

Ingredients:

- 5 lb. prime rib, sliced
- 2 tablespoons olive oil
- Salt and pepper to taste
- 8 cloves garlic
- 2 tablespoons rosemary, chopped
- 16 oz. mushrooms, sliced
- 1 cup chicken broth
- ¾ cup red wine
- 1 tablespoon mustard
- 1 teaspoon cornstarch
- 2 teaspoons water

Instructions:

1. Preheat your oven to 250 degrees F.

2. Coat the prime rib slices with oil.

3. Season with the salt and pepper.

4. Roast in the oven for 30 minutes.

5. Transfer to a plate.

6. Let cool.

7. Next, rub the rosemary and garlic on all sides of the steak.

8. Add the beef drippings from the baking pan to a pan over medium heat.

9. Add the rest of the ingredients.

10. Simmer for 5 minutes.

11. Add the mixture to the baking pan.

12. Lastly, bake in the oven for another 15 minutes.

Nutrients per Serving:

- Calories: 354.6
- Fat: 17.8 g
- Saturated Fat: 6.1 g
- Carbohydrates: 6 g
- Fiber: 1.8 g
- Protein: 36.4 g
- Cholesterol: 98.6 mg
- Sugars: 0.3 g
- Sodium: 1151.2 mg
- Potassium: 564.9 mg

Steak with Broccoli Rabe Peas

Ready in less than 30 minutes, this steak recipe is bound to impress everyone at the dinner table.

Serving Size: 4

Preparation Cooking Time: 25 minutes

Ingredients:

- 12 oz. beef top sirloin steak
- 2 teaspoons steak seasoning
- 2 teaspoons vegetable oil
- 6 oz. broccoli rabe
- 2 cups peas
- 3 cups mushrooms, sliced
- 1 tablespoon mustard
- 1 cup beef broth
- Salt to taste
- 2 teaspoons cornstarch

Instructions:

1. Preheat your oven to 350 degrees F.

2. Season the steak with the steak seasoning.

3. Next, add the oil to a pan over medium high heat.

4. Cook the broccoli rabe and steak for 4 to 5 minutes.

5. Sprinkle the peas around the steak.

6. Transfer to the oven. Then, bake for 8 to 10 minutes.

7. In a pan, simmer the remaining ingredients for 10 minutes.

8. Lastly, pour the sauce over the steak and veggies before serving.

Nutrients per Serving:

- Calories: 226
- Fat: 6.4 g
- Saturated fat: 1.5 g
- Carbohydrates: 16.4 g
- Fiber: 5.1 g
- Protein: 26.5 g
- Cholesterol: 51 mg
- Sugars: 6 g
- Sodium: 356 mg
- Potassium: 780 mg

Flank Steak with Tomato Salad

Grilled flank steak served with tomato salad on the side can certainly turn things around on an ordinary night at home.

Serving Size: 4

Preparation Cooking Time: 20 minutes

Ingredients:

- 2 cups cherry tomatoes, sliced in half
- 2 teaspoons garlic, chopped
- 1 jalapeño pepper, sliced
- ½ cup cilantro, chopped
- ½ cup olive oil
- Salt and pepper to taste
- 1 lb. flank steak, sliced

Instructions:

1. Preheat your grill.

2. In a bowl, mix the tomatoes, garlic, jalapeño pepper and cilantro.

3. Drizzle with the olive oil.

4. Toss to coat evenly.

5. Next, sprinkle both sides of the steaks with the salt and pepper.

6. Grill for 3 to 5 minutes per side.

7. Serve the steaks with tomato salad.

Nutrients per Serving:

- Calories: 346
- Fat: 25.1 g
- Saturated fat: 5 g
- Carbohydrates: 3.9 g
- Fiber: 1.1 g
- Protein: 25.3 g
- Cholesterol: 70 mg
- Sugars: 2 g
- Sodium: 358 mg
- Potassium: 591 mg

Herbed Steak with Tomatoes

If you're actually looking for a change in your weekly menu, try preparing this herbed steak topped with chopped tomatoes and green onion. It's flavorful, juicy and easy to make.

Serving Size: 2

Preparation Cooking Time: 30 minutes

Ingredients:

- 8 oz. beef top loin steak, sliced
- Salt and pepper to taste
- Cooking spray
- 1 teaspoon fresh basil, chopped
- ¼ cup green onions, chopped
- 1 cup tomato, chopped

Instructions:

1. First, season the steaks with the salt and pepper.

2. Spray your pan with oil.

3. Cook the steaks for 5 to 7 minutes per side.

4. Add the basil and green onions to the pan.

5. Next, cook for 2 minutes.

6. Add the tomatoes.

7. Cook for 1 minute.

8. Top the steaks with tomato and herbs.

Nutrients per Serving:

- Calories: 170
- Fat: 6 g
- Saturated fat: 2 g
- Carbohydrates: 3 g
- Fiber: 1 g
- Protein: 25 g
- Cholesterol: 66 mg
- Sugars: 2 g
- Sodium: 207 mg
- Potassium: 445 mg

Seared Steak with Crispy Herbs

Sear the steaks in your pan over high heat, flavor these up with herbs and serve with salad, rice or pasta.

Serving Size: 4

Preparation Cooking Time: 20 minutes

Ingredients:

- 1 sprig fresh rosemary, chopped
- 3 sprigs fresh sage, chopped
- 5 sprigs fresh thyme, chopped
- 1 lb. sirloin steak
- Salt and pepper to taste
- 2 tablespoons vegetable oil
- 4 cloves garlic, crushed

Instructions:

1. First, season your steak with the salt and pepper.

2. Add the steak to a pan over high heat.

3. Next, sear for 1 minute per side.

4. Add the oil, garlic and herbs to the pan.

5. Reduce heat and cook for 3 minutes per side.

Nutrients per Serving:

- Calories: 244
- Fat: 11.8 g
- Saturated fat: 2.5 g
- Carbohydrates: 10 g
- Fiber: 8.2 g
- Protein: 25.5 g
- Cholesterol: 59 mg
- Sugars: 1 g
- Sodium: 394 mg
- Potassium: 1111 mg

Flank Steak with Corn Butter

Everyone will rave about this combination—grilled flank steak, herbed butter and grilled corn.

Serving Size: 4

Preparation Cooking Time: 40 minutes

Ingredients:

- 4 tablespoons butter
- 2 tablespoons fresh chives, chopped
- 2 tablespoons fresh parsley, chopped
- 2 tablespoons fresh basil, chopped
- 1 tablespoon fresh thyme, chopped
- 1 tablespoon lemon juice
- Salt and pepper to taste
- 1 lb. flank steak, sliced
- 1 tablespoon oil
- 4 ears corn
- ¼ cup feta cheese, crumbled

Instructions:

1. Preheat your grill.

2. Add the butter, herbs, lemon juice, salt and pepper to a food processor.

3. Pulse until smooth.

4. Coat the steak with oil.

5. Sprinkle with the salt and pepper.

6. Grill the steak approximately for 4 to 5 minutes per side.

7. Top the steak with half of the herbed butter.

8. Grill the corn for 8 minutes, rotating often.

9. Spread the remaining butter on the corn.

10. Serve the steak with the grilled corn and feta cheese.

Nutrients per Serving:

- Calories: 420
- Fat: 26.3 g
- Saturated fat: 12.6 g
- Carbohydrates: 20.3 g
- Fiber: 2.3 g
- Protein: 29.3 g
- Cholesterol: 107 mg
- Sugars: 7 g
- Sodium: 730 mg
- Potassium: 590 mg

Conclusion

With this awesome lineup of steak dishes, expect to have a lot of fun in the kitchen.

All these will give you spectacular steak dishes without requiring you to spend too much time cooking.

Make sure that you choose high quality steaks and follow the recipes closely to get the results you're looking for.

Have fun!

About the Author

A native of Albuquerque, New Mexico, Sophia Freeman found her calling in the culinary arts when she enrolled at the Sante Fe School of Cooking. Freeman decided to take a year after graduation and travel around Europe, sampling the cuisine from small bistros and family owned restaurants from Italy to Portugal. Her bubbly personality and inquisitive nature made her popular with the locals in the villages and when she finished her trip and came home, she had made friends for life in the places she had visited. She also came home with a deeper understanding of European cuisine.

Freeman went to work at one of Albuquerque's 5-star restaurants as a sous-chef and soon worked her way up to head chef. The restaurant began to feature Freeman's original dishes as specials on the menu and soon after, she began to write e-books with her recipes. Sophia's dishes mix local flavours with European inspiration making them irresistible to the diners in her restaurant and the online community.

 Freeman's experience in Europe didn't just teach her new ways of cooking, but also unique methods of presentation. Using rich sauces, crisp vegetables and meat cooked to perfection, she creates a stunning display as well as a delectable dish. She has won many local awards for her cuisine and she continues to delight her diners with her culinary masterpieces.

★ ★ ★ ★ ★ ★ ★ ★ ★ ★ ★ ★ ★

Author's Afterthoughts

I want to convey my big thanks to all of my readers who have taken the time to read my book. Readers like you make my work so rewarding and I cherish each and every one of you.

Grateful cannot describe how I feel when I know that someone has chosen my work over all of the choices available online. I hope you enjoyed the book as much as I enjoyed writing it.

Feedback from my readers is how I grow and learn as a chef and an author. Please take the time to let me know your thoughts by leaving a review on Amazon so I and your fellow readers can learn from your experience.

My deepest thanks,

Sophia Freeman

https://sophia.subscribemenow.com/

Printed in Great Britain
by Amazon